Oliver Wendell Holmes

Before the Curfew

And Other Poems

Oliver Wendell Holmes

Before the Curfew
And Other Poems

ISBN/EAN: 9783744705257

Printed in Europe, USA, Canada, Australia, Japan

Cover: Foto ©Thomas Meinert / pixelio.de

More available books at **www.hansebooks.com**

By the Same Author.

POEMS. *Household Edition.* With Portrait. 12mo, $1.75; full gilt, $2.25.
Family Edition. Illustrated. 8vo, $2.50.
Handy-Volume Edition. With Portrait. 2 vols. 32mo, $2.50.
Illustrated Library Edition. With Illustrations and Portrait. 8vo, $3.50.
BEFORE THE CURFEW. 16mo, $1.25.
SONGS IN MANY KEYS. 16mo, $1.50.
ASTRÆA: The Balance of Illusions. 16mo, 75 cents.
SONGS OF MANY SEASONS. 16mo, $2.00.
THE SCHOOL-BOY. Illustrated. 4to, $2.50.
THE IRON GATE, and other Poems. With Portrait. 12mo, $1.25.
ILLUSTRATED POEMS. With etched Portrait and Illustrations. Royal 8vo, $4.00.
THE LAST LEAF. With twenty full-page phototypes, and other decorations. Quarto, $10.00.
GRANDMOTHER'S STORY, etc. 16mo, paper, 15 cents.
THE AUTOCRAT OF THE BREAKFAST-TABLE. With Portrait. Crown 8vo, $2.00.
Handy-Volume Edition. 32mo, $1.25.
THE PROFESSOR AT THE BREAKFAST-TABLE. Crown 8vo, $2.00.
THE POET AT THE BREAKFAST-TABLE. Crown 8vo, $2.00.
ELSIE VENNER. Crown 8vo, $2.00.
THE GUARDIAN ANGEL. A Novel. Crown 8vo, $2.00.
PAGES FROM AN OLD VOLUME OF LIFE. Crown 8vo, $2.00.
A MORTAL ANTIPATHY. Crown 8vo, $1.50.
OUR HUNDRED DAYS IN EUROPE. Crown 8vo, $1.50.
MEDICAL ESSAYS. Crown 8vo, $2.00.
THE BREAKFAST-TABLE SERIES, together with Elsie Venner, The Guardian Angel, Pages from an Old Volume of Life, A Mortal Antipathy, Medical Essays, Our Hundred Days in Europe, and Poems (*Household Edition*). 10 vols. $17.00.
JOHN LOTHROP MOTLEY. 16mo, $1.50.
RALPH WALDO EMERSON. With Portrait. 16mo, $1.25.

HOUGHTON, MIFFLIN & COMPANY,
BOSTON AND NEW YORK.

BEFORE THE CURFEW
AND OTHER POEMS, CHIEFLY OCCASIONAL

BY

OLIVER WENDELL HOLMES

BOSTON AND NEW YORK
HOUGHTON, MIFFLIN AND COMPANY
The Riverside Press, Cambridge
1888

Copyright, 1883,
BY OLIVER WENDELL HOLMES.

All rights reserved.

The Riverside Press, Cambridge:
Electrotyped and Printed by H. O. Houghton & Co.

AT MY FIRESIDE.

Alone, beneath the darkened sky,
  With saddened heart and unstrung lyre,
I heap the spoils of years gone by,
And leave them with a long-drawn sigh,
Like drift-wood brands that glimmering lie,
  Before the ashes hide the fire.

Let not these slow declining days
  The rosy light of dawn outlast;
Still round my lonely hearth it plays,
And gilds the east with borrowed rays,
While memory's mirrored sunset blaze
  Flames on the windows of the past.

March 1, 1888.

CONTENTS.

NOTE. — The poems marked thus, 1829–1882, etc., were written for and read at the annual meetings of the class which graduated at Harvard University in 1829.

	PAGE
BEFORE THE CURFEW	1
A LOVING-CUP SONG	6
THE GIRDLE OF FRIENDSHIP	8
THE LYRE OF ANACREON	10
THE OLD TUNE	13
THE BROKEN CIRCLE	15
THE ANGEL-THIEF	18
AT THE SATURDAY CLUB	20
BENJAMIN PEIRCE	27
OUR DEAD SINGER	29
TO JAMES FREEMAN CLARKE	31
TWO POEMS TO HARRIET BEECHER STOWE ON HER SEVENTIETH BIRTHDAY.	
I. AT THE SUMMIT	33
II. THE WORLD'S HOMAGE	34
A WELCOME TO DR. BENJAMIN APTHORP GOULD	37
TO FREDERICK HENRY HEDGE	40
TO JAMES RUSSELL LOWELL	42

CONTENTS.

To John Greenleaf Whittier	45
Prelude to a Volume printed in Raised Letters for the Blind	46
Boston to Florence	48
At the Unitarian Festival	49
Poem for the Two Hundred and Fiftieth Anniversary of the Founding of Harvard College	50
Post-Prandial	69
The Flaneur	72
Ave	78
King's Chapel. Read at the Two Hundredth Anniversary	80
Hymn for the same Occasion	84
Hymn. — The Word of Promise	86
Hymn Read at the Dedication of the Oliver Wendell Holmes Hospital at Hudson, Wisconsin, June 7, 1887	88
On the Death of President Garfield	90
The Golden Flower	94
No Time like the Old Time	96
The Morning Visit	98
Hail, Columbia!	103
Poem for the Dedication of the Fountain at Stratford-on-Avon, presented by George W. Childs, of Philadelphia	106
To the Poets who only Read and Listen	110

BEFORE THE CURFEW

AND OTHER POEMS.

BEFORE THE CURFEW.

1829–1882.

Not bed-time yet! The night-winds blow,
The stars are out, — full well we know
  The nurse is on the stair,
With hand of ice and cheek of snow,
And frozen lips that whisper low,
"Come, children, it is time to go
  My peaceful couch to share."

No years a wakeful heart can tire;
Not bed-time yet! Come, stir the fire
  And warm your dear old hands;
Kind Mother Earth we love so well
Has pleasant stories yet to tell
Before we hear the curfew bell;
  Still glow the burning brands.

Not bed-time yet! We long to know
What wonders time has yet to show,
  What unborn years shall bring;

What ship the Arctic pole shall reach,
What lessons Science waits to teach,
What sermons there are left to preach,
   What poems yet to sing.

What next? we ask; and is it true
The sunshine falls on nothing new,
   As Israel's king declared?
Was ocean ploughed with harnessed fire?
Were nations coupled with a wire?
Did Tarshish telegraph to Tyre?
   How Hiram would have stared!

And what if Sheba's curious queen,
Who came to see, — and to be seen, —
   Or something new to seek,
And swooned, as ladies sometimes do,
At sights that thrilled her through and through,
Had heard, as she was "coming to,"
   A locomotive's shriek,

And seen a rushing railway train
As she looked out along the plain
   From David's lofty tower, —
A mile of smoke that blots the sky
And blinds the eagles as they fly
Behind the cars that thunder by
   A score of leagues an hour!

See to my *fiat lux* respond
This little slumbering fire-tipped wand, —
  One touch, — it bursts in flame !
Steal me a portrait from the sun, —
One look, — and lo ! the picture done !
Are these old tricks, King Solomon,
  We lying moderns claim ?

Could you have spectroscoped a star ?
If both those mothers at your bar,
  The cruel and the mild,
The young and tender, old and tough,
Had said, "Divide, — you 're right, though rough," —
Did old Judea know enough
  To etherize the child ?

These births of time our eyes have seen,
With but a few brief years between ;
  What wonder if the text,
For other ages doubtless true,
For coming years will never do, —
Whereof we all should like a few
  If but to see what next.

If such things have been, such may be ;
Who would not like to live and see —
  If Heaven may so ordain —
What waifs undreamed of, yet in store,
The waves that roll forevermore

On life's long beach may cast ashore
From out the mist-clad main?

Will Earth to pagan dreams return
To find from misery's painted urn
   That all save hope has flown, —
Of Book and Church and Priest bereft,
The Rock of Ages vainly cleft,
Life's compass gone, its anchor left,
   Left, — lost, — in depths unknown?

Shall Faith the trodden path pursue
The *crux ansata* wearers knew
   Who sleep with folded hands,
Where, like a naked, lidless eye,
The staring Nile rolls wondering by
Those mountain slopes that climb the sky
   Above the drifting sands?

Or shall a nobler Faith return,
Its fanes a purer gospel learn,
   With holier anthems ring,
And teach us that our transient creeds
Were but the perishable seeds
Of harvests sown for larger needs
   That ripening years shall bring?

Well, let the present do its best,
We trust our Maker for the rest,
   As on our way we plod;

Our souls, full dressed in fleshly suits,
Love air and sunshine, flowers and fruits,
The daisies better than their roots
  Beneath the grassy sod.

Not bed-time yet! The full-blown flower
Of all the year — this evening hour —
  With friendship's flame is bright;
Life still is sweet, the heavens are fair,
Though fields are brown and woods are bare,
And many a joy is left to share
  Before we say Good-night!

And when, our cheerful evening past,
The nurse, long waiting, comes at last,
  Ere on her lap we lie
In wearied nature's sweet repose,
At peace with all her waking foes,
Our lips shall murmur, ere they close,
  Good-night! and not Good-by!

A LOVING-CUP SONG.

1829–1883.

Come, heap the fagots! Ere we go
Again the cheerful hearth shall glow;
 We 'll have another blaze, my boys!
When clouds are black and snows are white,
Then Christmas logs lend ruddy light
 They stole from summer days, my boys,
  They stole from summer days.

And let the Loving-Cup go round,
The Cup with blessed memories crowned,
 That flows whene'er we meet, my boys;
No draught will hold a drop of sin
If love is only well stirred in
 To keep it sound and sweet, my boys,
  To keep it sound and sweet.

Give me, to pin upon my breast,
The blossoms twain I love the best,
 A rosebud and a pink, my boys;
Their leaves shall nestle next my heart,
Their perfumed breath shall own its part
 In every health we drink, my boys,
  In every health we drink.

The breathing blossoms stir my blood,
Methinks I see the lilacs bud
    And hear the bluebirds sing, my boys;
Why not? Yon lusty oak has seen
Full tenscore years, yet leaflets green
      Peep out with every spring, my boys,
        Peep out with every spring.

Old Time his rusty scythe may whet,
The unmowed grass is glowing yet
    Beneath the sheltering snow, my boys;
And if the crazy dotard ask,
Is love worn out? Is life a task?
      We'll bravely answer No! my boys,
        We'll bravely answer No!

For life's bright taper is the same
Love tipped of old with rosy flame
    That heaven's own altar lent, my boys,
To glow in every cup we fill
Till lips are mute and hearts are still,
      Till life and love are spent, my boys,
        Till life and love are spent.

THE GIRDLE OF FRIENDSHIP.

1829–1884.

She gathered at her slender waist
    The beauteous robe she wore;
Its folds a golden belt embraced,
    One rose-hued gem it bore.

The girdle shrank; its lessening round
    Still kept the shining gem,
But now her flowing locks it bound,
    A lustrous diadem.

And narrower still the circlet grew;
    Behold! a glittering band,
Its roseate diamond set anew,
    Her neck's white column spanned.

Suns rise and set; the straining clasp
    The shortened links resist,
Yet flashes in a bracelet's grasp
    The diamond, on her wrist.

At length, the round of changes past
    The thieving years could bring,
The jewel, glittering to the last,
    Still sparkles in a ring.

So, link by link, our friendships part,
So loosen, break, and fall,
A narrowing zone; the loving heart
Lives changeless through them all.

THE LYRE OF ANACREON.
1829–1885.

The minstrel of the classic lay
    Of love and wine who sings
Still found the fingers run astray
    That touched the rebel strings.

Of Cadmus he would fain have sung,
    Of Atreus and his line;
But all the jocund echoes rung
    With songs of love and wine.

Ah, brothers! I would fain have caught
    Some fresher fancy's gleam;
My truant accents find, unsought,
    The old familiar theme.

Love, Love! but not the sportive child
    With shaft and twanging bow,
Whose random arrows drove us wild
    Some threescore years ago;

Not Eros, with his joyous laugh,
    The urchin blind and bare,
But Love, with spectacles and staff,
    And scanty, silvered hair.

Our heads with frosted locks are white,
   Our roofs are thatched with snow,
But red, in chilling winter's spite,
   Our hearts and hearthstones glow.

Our old acquaintance, Time, drops in,
   And while the running sands
Their golden thread unheeded spin,
   He warms his frozen hands.

Stay, wingëd hours, too swift, too sweet,
   And waft this message o'er
To all we miss, from all we meet
   On life's fast-crumbling shore:

Say that, to old affection true,
   We hug the narrowing chain
That binds our hearts, — alas, how few
   The links that yet remain!

The fatal touch awaits them all
   That turns the rocks to dust;
From year to year they break and fall, —
   They break, but never rust.

Say if one note of happier strain
   This worn-out harp afford, —
One throb that trembles, not in vain, —
   Their memory lent its chord.

Say that when Fancy closed her wings
And Passion quenched his fire,
Love, Love, still echoed from the strings
As from Anacreon's lyre!

THE OLD TUNE.

THIRTY-SIXTH VARIATION.

1829–1886.

THIS shred of song you bid me bring
   Is snatched from fancy's embers;
Ah, when the lips forget to sing,
   The faithful heart remembers!

Too swift the wings of envious Time
   To wait for dallying phrases,
Or woven strands of labored rhyme
   To thread their cunning mazes.

A word, a sigh, and lo, how plain
   Its magic breath discloses
Our life's long vista through a lane
   Of threescore summers' roses!

One language years alone can teach:
   Its roots are young affections
That feel their way to simplest speech
   Through silent recollections.

That tongue is ours. How few the words
   We need to know a brother!

As simple are the notes of birds,
  Yet well they know each other.

This freezing month of ice and snow
  That brings our lives together
Lends to our year a living glow
  That warms its wintry weather.

So let us meet as eve draws nigh,
  And life matures and mellows,
Till Nature whispers with a sigh,
  " Good-night, my dear old fellows ! "

THE BROKEN CIRCLE.

1829–1887.

I stood on Sarum's treeless plain,
    The waste that careless Nature owns;
Lone tenants of her bleak domain,
    Loomed huge and gray the Druid stones.

Upheaved in many a billowy mound
    The sea-like, naked turf arose,
Where wandering flocks went nibbling round
    The mingled graves of friends and foes.

The Briton, Roman, Saxon, Dane,
    This windy desert roamed in turn;
Unmoved these mighty blocks remain
    Whose story none that lives may learn.

Erect, half buried, slant or prone,
    These awful listeners, blind and dumb,
Hear the strange tongues of tribes unknown,
    As wave on wave they go and come.

"Who are you, giants, whence and why?"
    I stand and ask in blank amaze;
My soul accepts their mute reply:
    "A mystery, as are you that gaze.

"A silent Orpheus wrought the charm
    From riven rocks their spoils to bring;
A nameless Titan lent his arm
    To range us in our magic ring.

"But Time with still and stealthy stride,
    That climbs and treads and levels all,
That bids the loosening keystone slide,
    And topples down the crumbling wall, —

"Time, that unbuilds the quarried past,
    Leans on these wrecks that press the sod;
They slant, they stoop, they fall at last,
    And strew the turf their priests have trod.

"No more our altar's wreath of smoke
    Floats up with morning's fragrant dew;
The fires are dead, the ring is broke,
    Where stood the many stand the few."

— My thoughts had wandered far away,
    Borne off on Memory's outspread wing,
To where in deepening twilight lay
    The wrecks of friendship's broken ring.

Ah me! of all our goodly train
    How few will find our banquet hall!
Yet why with coward lips complain
    That this must lean, and that must fall?

THE BROKEN CIRCLE.

Cold is the Druid's altar-stone,
  Its vanished flame no more returns ;
But ours no chilling damp has known, —
  Unchanged, unchanging, still it burns.

So let our broken circle stand
  A wreck, a remnant, yet the same,
While one last, loving, faithful hand
  Still lives to feed its altar-flame!

THE ANGEL-THIEF.

1829–1888.

Time is a thief who leaves his tools behind him;
   He comes by night, he vanishes at dawn;
We track his footsteps, but we never find him:
   Strong locks are broken, massive bolts are drawn,

And all around are left the bars and borers,
   The splitting wedges and the prying keys,
Such aids as serve the soft-shod vault-explorers
   To crack, wrench open, rifle as they please.

Ah, these are tools which Heaven in mercy lends us!
   When gathering rust has clenched our shackles fast,
Time is the angel-thief that Nature sends us
   To break the cramping fetters of our past.

Mourn as we may for treasures he has taken,
   Poor as we feel of hoarded wealth bereft,
More precious are those implements forsaken,
   Found in the wreck his ruthless hands have left.

Some lever that a casket's hinge has broken
  Pries off a bolt, and lo! our souls are free;
Each year some Open Sesame is spoken,
  And every decade drops its master-key.

So as from year to year we count our treasures,
  Our loss seems less, and larger look our gains;
Time's wrongs repaid in more than even measure, —
  We lose our jewels, but we break our chains.

AT THE SATURDAY CLUB.

This is our place of meeting; opposite
That towered and pillared building: look at it;
King's Chapel in the Second George's day,
Rebellion stole its regal name away, —
Stone Chapel sounded better; but at last
The poisoned name of our provincial past
Had lost its ancient venom; then once more
Stone Chapel was King's Chapel as before.
(So let rechristened North Street, when it can,
Bring back the days of Marlborough and Queen
    Anne!)
  Next the old church your wandering eye will
    meet
A granite pile that stares upon the street, —
Our civic temple; slanderous tongues have said
Its shape was modelled from Saint Botolph's
    head,
Lofty, but narrow; jealous passers-by
Say Boston always held her head too high.
  Turn half-way round, and let your look survey
The white façade that gleams across the way, —
The many-windowed building, tall and wide,
The palace-inn that shows its northern side
In grateful shadow when the sunbeams beat

The granite wall in summer's scorching heat.
This is the place; whether its name you spell
Tavern, or caravansera, or hotel.
Would I could steal its echoes! you should find
Such store of vanished pleasures brought to mind:
Such feasts! the laughs of many a jocund hour
That shook the mortar from King George's
    tower;
Such guests! What famous names its record
    boasts,
Whose owners wander in the mob of ghosts!
Such stories! every beam and plank is filled
With juicy wit the joyous talkers spilled,
Ready to ooze, as once the mountain pine
The floors are laid with oozed its turpentine!

A month had flitted since The Club had met;
The day came round; I found the table set,
The waiters lounging round the marble stairs,
Empty as yet the double row of chairs.
I was a full half hour before the rest,
Alone, the banquet-chamber's single guest.
So from the table's side a chair I took,
And having neither company nor book
To keep me waking, by degrees there crept
A torpor over me, — in short, I slept.
    Loosed from its chain, along the wreck-strown
        track
Of the dead years my soul goes travelling back;
My ghosts take on their robes of flesh; it seems

Dreaming is life ; nay, life less life than dreams,
So real are the shapes that meet my eyes. —
They bring no sense of wonder, no surprise,
No hint of other than an earth-born source ;
All seems plain daylight, everything of course.
  How dim the colors are, how poor and faint
This palette of weak words with which I paint !
Here sit my friends ; if I could fix them so
As to my eyes they seem, my page would glow
Like a queen's missal, warm as if the brush
Of Titian or Velasquez brought the flush
Of life into their features. *Ay de mi!*
If syllables were pigments, you should see
Such breathing portraitures as never man
Found in the Pitti or the Vatican.

  Here sits our POET, Laureate, if you will,
Long has he worn the wreath, and wears it still.
Dead? Nay, not so ; and yet they say his bust
Looks down on marbles covering royal dust,
Kings by the Grace of God, or Nature's grace ;
Dead! No! Alive! I see him in his place,
Full-featured, with the bloom that heaven denies
Her children, pinched by cold New England
      skies,
Too often, while the nursery's happier few
Win from a summer cloud its roseate hue.
Kind, soft-voiced, gentle, in his eye there shines
The ray serene that filled Evangeline's.
  Modest he seems, not shy ; content to wait

Amid the noisy clamor of debate
The looked-for moment when a peaceful word
Smooths the rough ripples louder tongues have
    stirred.
In every tone I mark his tender grace
And all his poems hinted in his face;
What tranquil joy his friendly presence gives!
How could I think him dead? He lives! He
    lives!

  There, at the table's further end I see
In his old place our Poet's *vis-à-vis*,
The great PROFESSOR, strong, broad-shouldered,
    square,
In life's rich noontide, joyous, debonair.
His social hour no leaden care alloys,
His laugh rings loud and mirthful as a boy's, —
That lusty laugh the Puritan forgot, —
What ear has heard it and remembers not?
How often, halting at some wide crevasse
Amid the windings of his Alpine pass,
High up the cliffs, the climbing mountaineer,
Listening the far-off avalanche to hear,
Silent, and leaning on his steel-shod staff,
Has heard that cheery voice, that ringing laugh,
From the rude cabin whose nomadic walls
Creep with the moving glacier as it crawls!

  How does vast Nature lead her living train
In ordered sequence through that spacious brain,
As in the primal hour when Adam named

The new-born tribes that young creation
    claimed! —
How will her realm be darkened, losing thee,
Her darling, whom we call *our* AGASSIZ!

But who is he whose massive frame belies
The maiden shyness of his downcast eyes?
Who broods in silence till, by questions pressed,
Some answer struggles from his laboring breast?
An artist Nature meant to dwell apart,
Locked in his studio with a human heart,
Tracking its caverned passions to their lair,
And all its throbbing mysteries laying bare.
  Count it no marvel that he broods alone
Over the heart he studies, — 't is his own;
So in his page whatever shape it wear,
The Essex wizard's shadowed self is there, —
The great ROMANCER, hid beneath his veil
Like the stern preacher of his sombre tale;
Virile in strength, yet bashful as a girl,
Prouder than Hester, sensitive as Pearl.

From his mild throng of worshippers released,
Our Concord Delphi sends its chosen priest,
Prophet or poet, mystic, sage, or seer,
By every title always welcome here.
Why that ethereal spirit's frame describe?
You know the race-marks of the Brahmin tribe, —
The spare, slight form, the sloping shoulders'
    droop,

The calm, scholastic mien, the clerkly stoop,
The lines of thought the sharpened features wear,
Carved by the edge of keen New England air.
   List! for he speaks! As when a king would
      choose
The jewels for his bride, he might refuse
This diamond for its flaw, — find that less bright
Than those, its fellows, and a pearl less white
Than fits her snowy neck, and yet at last,
The fairest gems are chosen, and made fast
In golden fetters; so, with light delays
He seeks the fittest word to fill his phrase;
Nor vain nor idle his fastidious quest,
His chosen word is sure to prove the best.
   Where in the realm of thought, whose air is
      song,
Does he, the Buddha of the West, belong?
He seems a wingèd Franklin, sweetly wise,
Born to unlock the secrets of the skies;
And which the nobler calling, — if 't is fair
Terrestrial with celestial to compare, —
To guide the storm-cloud's elemental flame,
Or walk the chambers whence the lightning came,
Amidst the sources of its subtile fire,
And steal their effluence for his lips and lyre?
   If lost at times in vague aerial flights,
None treads with firmer footstep when he lights;
A soaring nature, ballasted with sense,
Wisdom without her wrinkles or pretence,
In every Bible he has faith to read,

And every altar helps to shape his creed.
Ask you what name this prisoned spirit bears
While with ourselves this fleeting breath it shares?
Till angels greet him with a sweeter one
In heaven, on earth we call him EMERSON.

  I start; I wake; the vision is withdrawn;
Its figures fading like the stars at dawn;
Crossed from the roll of life their cherished names,
And memory's pictures fading in their frames;
Yet life is lovelier for these transient gleams
Of buried friendships; blest is he who dreams!

BENJAMIN PEIRCE:

ASTRONOMER, MATHEMATICIAN.

1809–1880.

For him the Architect of all
Unroofed our planet's starlit hall;
Through voids unknown to worlds unseen
His clearer vision rose serene.

With us on earth he walked by day,
His midnight path how far away!
We knew him not so well who knew
The patient eyes his soul looked through;

For who his untrod realm could share
Of us that breathe this mortal air,
Or camp in that celestial tent
Whose fringes gild our firmament?

How vast the workroom where he brought
The viewless implements of thought!
The wit how subtle, how profound,
That Nature's tangled webs unwound;

That through the clouded matrix saw
The crystal planes of shaping law,

Through these the sovereign skill that planned, —
The Father's care, the Master's hand!

To him the wandering stars revealed
The secrets in their cradle sealed:
The far-off, frozen sphere that swings
Through ether, zoned with lucid rings;

The orb that rolls in dim eclipse
Wide wheeling round its long ellipse, —
His name Urania writes with these
And stamps it on her Pleiades.

We knew him not? Ah, well we knew
The manly soul, so brave, so true,
The cheerful heart that conquered age,
The childlike silver-bearded sage.

No more his tireless thought explores
The azure sea with golden shores;
Rest, wearied frame! the stars shall keep
A loving watch where thou shalt sleep.

Farewell! the spirit needs must rise,
So long a tenant of the skies, —
Rise to that home all worlds above
Whose sun is God, whose light is love.

OUR DEAD SINGER.

H. W. L.

Pride of the sister realm so long our own,
   We claim with her that spotless fame of thine,
   White as her snow and fragrant as her pine!
Ours was thy birthplace, but in every zone
Some wreath of song thy liberal hand has thrown
   Breathes perfume from its blossoms, that entwine
   Where'er the dewdrops fall, the sunbeams shine,
On life's long path with tangled cares o'ergrown.
Can Art thy truthful counterfeit command, —
   The silver-haloed features, tranquil, mild, —
   Soften the lips of bronze as when they smiled,
Give warmth and pressure to the marble hand?
Seek the lost rainbow in the sky it spanned!
   Farewell, sweet Singer! Heaven reclaims its child.

Carved from the block or cast in clinging mould,
   Will grateful Memory fondly try her best
   The mortal vesture from decay to wrest;

His look shall greet us, calm, but ah, how cold!
No breath can stir the brazen drapery's fold,
  No throb can heave the statue's stony breast;
  "He is not here, but risen," will stand confest
In all we miss, in all our eyes behold.
How Nature loved him! On his placid brow,
  Thought's ample dome, she set the sacred sign
  That marks the priesthood of her holiest shrine,
Nor asked a leaflet from the laurel's bough
That envious Time might clutch or disallow,
  To prove her chosen minstrel's song divine.

On many a saddened hearth the evening fire
  Burns paler as the children's hour draws near, —
  That joyous hour his song made doubly dear, —
And tender memories touch the faltering choir.
He sings no more on earth; our vain desire
  Aches for the voice we loved so long to hear
  In Dorian flute-notes breathing soft and clear, —
The sweet contralto that could never tire.
Deafened with listening to a harsher strain,
  The Mænad's scream, the stark barbarian's cry,
  Still for those soothing, loving tones we sigh;
Oh, for our vanished Orpheus once again!
The shadowy silence hears us call in vain!
  His lips are hushed; his song shall never die.

TO JAMES FREEMAN CLARKE.

APRIL 4, 1880.

I BRING the simplest pledge of love,
    Friend of my earlier days;
Mine is the hand without the glove,
    The heart-beat, not the phrase.

How few still breathe this mortal air
    We called by schoolboy names!
You still, whatever robe you wear,
    To me are always James:

That name the kind apostle bore
    Who shames the sullen creeds,
Not trusting less, but loving more,
    And showing faith by deeds.

What blending thoughts our memories share!
    What visions yours and mine
Of May-days in whose morning air
    The dews were golden wine;

Of vistas bright with opening day,
    Whose all-awakening sun
Showed in life's landscape, far away,
    The summits to be won!

The heights are gained. — Ah, say not so
   For him who smiles at time,
Leaves his tired comrades down below,
   And only lives to climb!

His labors, — will they ever cease,
   With hand, and tongue, and pen?
Shall wearied Nature ask release
   At threescore years and ten?

Our strength the clustered seasons tax, —
   For him new life they mean;
Like rods around the lictor's axe
   They keep him bright and keen.

The wise, the brave, the strong, we know, —
   We mark them here or there;
But he, — we roll our eyes, and lo!
   We find him everywhere!

With truth's bold cohorts, or alone,
   He strides through error's field;
His lance is ever manhood's own,
   His breast is woman's shield.

Count not his years while earth has need
   Of souls that Heaven inflames
With sacred zeal to save, to lead, —
   Long live our dear Saint James!

TWO POEMS TO HARRIET BEECHER STOWE

ON HER SEVENTIETH BIRTHDAY, JUNE 14, 1882.

I. AT THE SUMMIT.

SISTER, we bid you welcome, — we who stand
    On the high table-land;
We who have climbed life's slippery Alpine slope,
And rest, still leaning on the staff of hope,
Looking along the silent Mer de Glace,
Leading our footsteps where the dark crevasse
Yawns in the frozen sea we all must pass, —
    Sister, we clasp your hand!

Rest with us in the hour that Heaven has lent
    Before the swift descent.
Look! the warm sunbeams kiss the glittering ice;
See! next the snow-drift blooms the edelweiss;
The mated eagles fan the frosty air;
Life, beauty, love, around us everywhere,
And, in their time, the darkening hours that bear
    Sweet memories, peace, content.

Thrice welcome! shining names our missals show
    Amid their rubrics' glow,

But search the blazoned record's starry line,
What halo's radiance fills the page like thine?
Thou who by some celestial clew couldst find
The way to all the hearts of all mankind,
On thee, already canonized, enshrined,
    What more can Heaven bestow?

II. THE WORLD'S HOMAGE.

IF every tongue that speaks her praise
For whom I shape my tinkling phrase
    Were summoned to the table,
The vocal chorus that would meet
Of mingling accents harsh or sweet,
From every land and tribe, would beat
    The polyglots at Babel.

Briton and Frenchman, Swede and Dane,
Turk, Spaniard, Tartar of Ukraine,
    Hidalgo, Cossack, Cadi,
High Dutchman and Low Dutchman, too,
The Russian serf, the Polish Jew,
Arab, Armenian, and Mantchoo,
    Would shout, "We know the lady!"

. Know her! Who knows not Uncle Tom
And her he learned his gospel from
    Has never heard of Moses;
Full well the brave black hand we know

That gave to freedom's grasp the hoe
That killed the weed that used to grow
   Among the Southern roses.

When Archimedes, long ago,
Spoke out so grandly, "*Dos pou sto*, —
   Give me a place to stand on,
I'll move your planet for you, now," —
He little dreamed or fancied how
The *sto* at last should find its *pou*
   For woman's faith to land on.

Her lever was the wand of art,
Her fulcrum was the human heart,
   Whence all unfailing aid is;
She moved the earth! Its thunders pealed,
Its mountains shook, its temples reeled,
The blood-red fountains were unsealed,
   And Moloch sunk to Hades.

All through the conflict, up and down
Marched Uncle Tom and Old John Brown,
   One ghost, one form ideal;
And which was false and which was true,
And which was mightier of the two,
The wisest sibyl never knew,
   For both alike were real.

Sister, the holy maid does well
Who counts her beads in convent cell,
   Where pale devotion lingers;

But she who serves the sufferer's needs,
Whose prayers are spelt in loving deeds,
May trust the Lord will count her beads
   As well as human fingers.

When Truth herself was Slavery's slave,
Thy hand the prisoned suppliant gave
   The rainbow wings of fiction.
And Truth who soared descends to-day
Bearing an angel's wreath away,
Its lilies at thy feet to lay
   With Heaven's own benediction.

A WELCOME TO DR. BENJAMIN APTHORP GOULD.

ON HIS RETURN FROM SOUTH AMERICA,

AFTER FIFTEEN YEARS DEVOTED TO CATALOGUING THE STARS OF THE SOUTHERN HEMISPHERE.[1]

Once more Orion and the sister Seven
   Look on thee from the skies that hailed thy birth, —
How shall we welcome thee, whose home was heaven,
   From thy celestial wanderings back to earth?

Science has kept her midnight taper burning
   To greet thy coming with its vestal flame;
Friendship has murmured, "When art thou returning?"
   "Not yet! Not yet!" the answering message came.

Thine was unstinted zeal, unchilled devotion,
   While the blue realm had kingdoms to explore, —

---

[1] Read at the Dinner given at the Hotel Vendome, May 6, 1885.

Patience, like his who ploughed the unfurrowed
    ocean,
  Till o'er its margin loomed San Salvador.

Through the long nights I see thee ever waking,
  Thy footstool earth, thy roof the hemisphere,
While with thy griefs our weaker hearts are aching,
  Firm as thine equatorial's rock-based pier.

The souls that voyaged the azure depths before
    thee
  Watch with thy tireless vigils, all unseen, —
Tycho and Kepler bend benignant o'er thee,
  And with his toy-like tube the Florentine, —

He at whose word the orb that bore him shivered
  To find her central sovereignty disowned,
While the wan lips of priest and pontiff quivered,
  Their jargon stilled, their Baal disenthroned.

Flamsteed and Newton look with brows unclouded,
  Their strife forgotten with its faded scars, —
(Titans, who found the world of space too crowded
  To walk in peace among its myriad stars.)

All cluster round thee, — seers of earliest ages,
  Persians, Ionians, Mizraim's learned kings,
From the dim days of Shinar's hoary sages
  To his who weighed the planet's fluid rings.

And we, for whom the northern heavens are
 lighted,
 For whom the storm has passed, the sun has
  smiled,
Our clouds all scattered, all our stars united,
 We claim thee, clasp thee, like a long-lost
  child.

Fresh from the spangled vault's o'erarching splen-
 dor,
 Thy lonely pillar, thy revolving dome,
In heartfelt accents, proud, rejoicing, tender,
 We bid thee welcome to thine earthly home!

TO FREDERICK HENRY HEDGE.

AT A DINNER GIVEN HIM ON HIS EIGHTIETH BIRTHDAY, DECEMBER 12, 1885.

With a bronze statuette of John of Bologna's Mercury, presented by a few friends.

FIT emblem for the altar's side,
    And him who serves its daily need,
The stay, the solace, and the guide
    Of mortal men, whate'er his creed!

Flamen or Auspex, Priest or Bonze,
    He feeds the upward-climbing fire,
Still teaching, like the deathless bronze,
    Man's noblest lesson, — to aspire.

Hermes lies prone by fallen Jove,
    Crushed are the wheels of Krishna's car,
And o'er Dodona's silent grove
    Streams the white ray from Bethlehem's star.

Yet snatched from Time's relentless clutch,
    A godlike shape, that human hands
Have fired with Art's electric touch,
    The herald of Olympus stands.

TO FREDERICK HENRY HEDGE.

Ask not what ore the furnace knew;
　　Love mingled with the flowing mass,
And lends its own unchanging hue,
　　Like gold in Corinth's molten brass.

Take then our gift; this airy form
　　Whose bronze our benedictions gild,
The hearts of all its givers warm
　　With love by freezing years unchilled.

With eye undimmed, with strength unworn,
　　Still toiling in your Master's field,
Before you wave the growths unshorn,
　　Their ripened harvest yet to yield.

True servant of the Heavenly Sire,
　　To you our tried affection clings,
Bids you still labor, still aspire,
　　But clasps your feet and steals their wings.

TO JAMES RUSSELL LOWELL.

This is your month, the mouth of "perfect days,"
Birds in full song and blossoms all ablaze.
Nature herself your earliest welcome breathes,
Spreads every leaflet, every bower inwreathes;
Carpets her paths for your returning feet,
Puts forth her best your coming steps to greet;
And Heaven must surely find the earth in tune
When Home, sweet Home, exhales the breath of June.
These blessed days are waning all too fast,
And June's bright visions mingling with the past;
Lilacs have bloomed and faded, and the rose
Has dropped its petals, but the clover blows,
And fills its slender tubes with honeyed sweets;
The fields are pearled with milk-white margarites;
The dandelion, which you sang of old,
Has lost its pride of place, its crown of gold,
But still displays its feathery-mantled globe,
Which children's breath, or wandering winds unrobe.
These were your humble friends; your opened eyes
Nature had trained her common gifts to prize;

Not Cam nor Isis taught you to despise
Charles, with his muddy margin and the harsh,
Plebeian grasses of the reeking marsh.
New England's home-bred scholar, well you knew
Her soil, her speech, her people, through and
through,
And loved them ever with the love that holds
All sweet, fond memories in its fragrant folds.
Though far and wide your wingëd words have
flown,
Your daily presence kept you all our own,
Till, with a sorrowing sigh, a thrill of pride,
We heard your summons, and you left our side
For larger duties and for tasks untried.

How pleased the Spaniards for a while to claim
This frank Hidalgo with the liquid name,
Who stored their classics on his crowded shelves
And loved their Calderon as they did themselves!
Before his eyes what changing pageants pass!
The bridal feast how near the funeral mass!
The death-stroke falls, — the Misereres wail;
The joy-bells ring, — the tear-stained cheeks unveil,
While, as the playwright shifts his pictured scene,
The royal mourner crowns his second queen.

From Spain to Britain is a goodly stride, —
Madrid and London long-stretched leagues divide.

What if I send him, "Uncle S., says he,"
To my good cousin whom he calls " J. B."?
A nation's servants go where they are sent, —
He heard his Uncle's orders, and he went.

By what enchantments, what alluring arts,
Our truthful James led captive British hearts, —
Whether his shrewdness made their statesmen halt,
Or if his learning found their Dons at fault,
Or if his virtue was a strange surprise,
Or if his wit flung star-dust in their eyes, —
Like honest Yankees we can simply guess;
But that he did it all must needs confess.
England herself without a blush may claim
Her only conqueror since the Norman came.

Eight years an exile! What a weary while
Since first our herald sought the mother isle!
His snow-white flag no churlish wrong has soiled, —
He left unchallenged, he returns unspoiled.

Here let us keep him, here he saw the light, —
His genius, wisdom, wit, are ours by right;
And if we lose him our lament will be
We have " five hundred " — *not* " as good as he."

TO JOHN GREENLEAF WHITTIER

ON HIS EIGHTIETH BIRTHDAY.

1887.

FRIEND, whom thy fourscore winters leave more dear
Than when life's roseate summer on thy cheek
Burned in the flush of manhood's manliest year,
Lonely, how lonely! is the snowy peak
Thy feet have reached, and mine have climbed so near!
Close on thy footsteps 'mid the landscape drear
I stretch my hand thine answering grasp to seek,
Warm with the love no rippling rhymes can speak!
Look backwards! From thy lofty height survey
Thy years of toil, of peaceful victories won,
Of dreams made real, largest hopes outrun!
Look forward! Brighter than earth's morning ray
Streams the pure light of Heaven's unsetting sun,
The unclouded dawn of life's immortal day!

PRELUDE TO A VOLUME PRINTED IN RAISED LETTERS FOR THE BLIND.

DEAR friends, left darkling in the long eclipse
That veils the noonday, — you whose finger-tips
A meaning in these ridgy leaves can find
Where ours go stumbling, senseless, helpless, blind,
This wreath of verse how dare I offer you
To whom the garden's choicest gifts are due?
The hues of all its glowing beds are ours, —
Shall you not claim its sweetest-smelling flowers?

Nay, those I have I bring you, — at their birth
Life's cheerful sunshine warmed the grateful earth;
If my rash boyhood dropped some idle seeds,
And here and there you light on saucy weeds
Among the fairer growths, remember still
Song comes of grace, and not of human will:
We get a jarring note when most we try,
Then strike the chord we know not how or why;
Our stately verse with too aspiring art
Oft overshoots and fails to reach the heart,
While the rude rhyme one human throb endears
Turns grief to smiles, and softens mirth to tears.

TO A VOLUME FOR THE BLIND.

Kindest of critics, ye whose fingers read,
From Nature's lesson learn the poet's creed;
The queenly tulip flaunts in robes of flame,
The wayside seedling scarce a tint may claim,
Yet may the lowliest leaflets that unfold
A dewdrop fresh from heaven's own chalice hold.

BOSTON TO FLORENCE.

SENT TO "THE PHILOLOGICAL CIRCLE" OF FLORENCE FOR ITS MEETING IN COMMEMORATION OF DANTE, JANUARY 27, 1881, ANNIVERSARY OF HIS FIRST CONDEMNATION.

PROUD of her clustering spires, her new-built towers,
    Our Venice, stolen from the slumbering sea,
    A sister's kindliest greeting wafts to thee,
Rose of Val d'Arno, Queen of all its flowers!
Thine exile's shrine thy sorrowing love embowers,
    Yet none with truer homage bends the knee,
    Or stronger pledge of fealty brings, than we,
Whose poets make thy dead Immortal ours.
Lonely the height, but ah, to heaven how near!
    Dante, whence flowed that solemn verse of thine
    Like the stern river from its Apennine
Whose name the far-off Scythian thrilled with fear:
Now to all lands thy deep-toned voice is dear,
    And every language knows the Song Divine!

AT THE UNITARIAN FESTIVAL.

MARCH 8, 1882.

The waves unbuild the wasting shore;
   Where mountains towered the billows sweep,
Yet still their borrowed spoils restore,
   And build new empires from the deep.
So while the floods of thought lay waste
   The proud domain of priestly creeds,
Its heaven-appointed tides will haste
   To plant new homes for human needs.
Be ours to mark with hearts unchilled
   The change an outworn church deplores;
The legend sinks, but Faith shall build
   A fairer throne on new-found shores.

POEM

FOR THE TWO HUNDRED AND FIFTIETH ANNIVERSARY OF THE FOUNDING OF HARVARD COLLEGE.

TWICE had the mellowing sun of autumn crowned
The hundredth circle of his yearly round,
When, as we meet to-day, our fathers met:
That joyous gathering who can e'er forget,
When Harvard's nurslings, scattered far and wide,
Through mart and village, lake's and ocean's side,
Came, with one impulse, one fraternal throng,
And crowned the hours with banquet, speech, and song?

Once more revived in fancy's magic glass,
I see in state the long procession pass:
Tall, courtly, leader as by right divine,
Winthrop, our Winthrop, rules the marshalled line,
Still seen in front, as on that far-off day
His ribboned baton showed the column's way.
Not all are gone who marched in manly pride
And waved their truncheons at their leader's side;

Gray, Lowell, Dixwell, who his empire shared,
These to be with us envious Time has spared.

Few are the faces, so familiar then,
Our eyes still meet amid the haunts of men;
Scarce one of all the living gathered there,
Whose unthinned locks betrayed a silver hair,
Greets us to-day, and yet we seem the same
As our own sires and grandsires, save in name.

There are the patriarchs, looking vaguely round
For classmates' faces, hardly known if found;
See the cold brow that rules the busy mart;
Close at its side the pallid son of art,
Whose purchased skill with borrowed meaning clothes,
And stolen hues, the smirking face he loathes.
Here is the patient scholar; in his looks
You read the titles of his learned books;
What classic lore those spidery crow's-feet speak!
What problems figure on that wrinkled cheek!
For never thought but left its stiffened trace,
Its fossil footprint, on the plastic face,
As the swift record of a raindrop stands,
Fixed on the tablet of the hardening sands.
On every face as on the written page
Each year renews the autograph of age;
One trait alone may wasting years defy, —
The fire still lingering in the poet's eye,
While Hope, the siren, sings her sweetest strain, —
Non omnis moriar is its proud refrain.

Sadly we gaze upon the vacant chair;
He who should claim its honors is not there, —
Otis, whose lips the listening crowd enthrall
That press and pack the floor of Boston's hall.
But Kirkland smiles, released from toil and care
Since the silk mantle younger shoulders wear, —
Quincy's, whose spirit breathes the selfsame fire
That filled the bosom of his youthful sire,
Who for the altar bore the kindled torch
To freedom's temple, dying in its porch.
  Three grave professions in their sons appear,
Whose words well studied all well pleased will
      hear:
Palfrey, ordained in varied walks to shine,
Statesman, historian, critic, and divine;
Solid and square behold majestic Shaw,
A mass of wisdom and a mine of law;
Warren, whose arm the doughtiest warriors fear,
Asks of the startled crowd to lend its ear, —
Proud of his calling, him the world loves best,
Not as the coming, but the parting guest.

Look on that form, — with eye dilating scan
The stately mould of nature's kingliest man!
Tower-like he stands in life's unfaded prime;
Ask you his name? None asks a second time!
He from the land his outward semblance takes,
Where storm-swept mountains watch o'er slum-
      bering lakes.
See in the impress which the body wears

How its imperial might the soul declares:
The forehead's large expansion, lofty, wide,
That locks unsilvered vainly strive to hide;
The lines of thought that plough the sober
    cheek;
Lips that betray their wisdom ere they speak
In tones like answers from Dodona's grove;
An eye like Juno's when she frowns on Jove.
I look and wonder; will he be content —
This man, this monarch, for the purple meant —
The meaner duties of his tribe to share,
Clad in the garb that common mortals wear?
Ah, wild Ambition, spread thy restless wings,
Beneath whose plumes the hidden œstrum stings;
Thou whose bold flight would leave earth's vul-
    gar crowds,
And like the eagle soar above the clouds,
Must feel the pang that fallen angels know
When the red lightning strikes thee from below!

Less bronze, more silver, mingles in the mould
Of him whom next my roving eyes behold;
His, more the scholar's than the statesman's face,
Proclaims him born of academic race.
Weary his look, as if an aching brain
Left on his brow the frozen prints of pain;
His voice far-reaching, grave, sonorous, owns
A shade of sadness in its plaintive tones,
Yet when its breath some loftier thought in-
    spires

Glows with a heat that every bosom fires.
Such Everett seems; no chance-sown wild flower
　　　knows
The full-blown charms of culture's double rose, —
Alas, how soon, by death's unsparing frost,
Its bloom is faded and its fragrance lost!

Two voices, only two, to earth belong,
Of all whose accents met the listening throng:
Winthrop, alike for speech and guidance framed,
On that proud day a twofold duty claimed;
One other yet, — remembered or forgot, —
Forgive my silence if I name him not.
Can I believe it? I, whose youthful voice
Claimed a brief gamut, — notes not over-
　　　choice, —
Stood undismayed before the solemn throng,
And *propria voce* sung that saucy song
Which even in memory turns my soul aghast, —
Felix audacia was the verdict cast.

What were the glory of these festal days
Shorn of their grand illumination's blaze?
Night comes at last with all her starry train
To find a light in every glittering pane.
From "Harvard's" windows see the sudden
　　　flash, —
Old "Massachusetts" glares through every sash;
From wall to wall the kindling splendors run
Till all is glorious as the noonday sun.

How to the scholar's mind each object brings
What some historian tells, some poet sings!
The good gray teacher whom we all revered —
Loved, honored, laughed at, and by freshman
    feared,
As from old "Harvard," where its light began,
From hall to hall the clustering splendors ran —
Took down his well-worn Æschylus and read,
Lit by the rays a thousand tapers shed,
How the swift herald crossed the leagues be-
    tween
Mycenæ's monarch and his faithless queen;
And thus he read, — my verse but ill displays
The Attic picture, clad in modern phrase:

On Ida's summit flames the kindling pile,
And Lemnos answers from his rocky isle;
From Athos next it climbs the reddening skies,
Thence where the watch-towers of Macistus rise.
The sentries of Mesapius in their turn
Bid the dry heath in high-piled masses burn,
Cithæron's crag the crimson billows stain,
Far Ægiplanctus joins the fiery train.
Thus the swift courier through the pathless night
Has gained at length the Arachnæan height,
Whence the glad tidings, borne on wings of flame,
"Ilium has fallen!" reach the royal dame.

So ends the day; before the midnight stroke
The lights expiring cloud the air with smoke;

While these the toil of younger hands employ,
The slumbering Grecian dreams of smouldering
    Troy.

As to that hour with backward steps I turn,
Midway I pause; behold a funeral urn!
Ah, sad memorial! known but all too well
The tale which thus its golden letters tell:

*This dust, once breathing, changed its joyous life
For toil and hunger, wounds and mortal strife;
Love, friendship, learning's all-prevailing
    charms,
For the cold bivouac and the clash of arms.
The cause of freedom won, a race enslaved
Called back to manhood, and a nation saved,
These sons of Harvard, falling ere their prime,
Leave their proud memory to the coming time.*

While in their still retreats our scholars turn
The mildewed pages of the past, to learn
With endless labor of the sleepless brain
What once has been and ne'er shall be again,
We reap the harvest of their ceaseless toil
And find a fragrance in their midnight oil.
But let a purblind mortal dare the task
The embryo future of itself to ask,
The world reminds him, with a scornful laugh,
That times have changed since Prospero broke
    his staff.

Could all the wisdom of the schools foretell
The dismal hour when Lisbon shook and fell,
Or name the shuddering night that toppled down
Our sister's pride, beneath whose mural crown
Scarce had the scowl forgot its angry lines,
When earth's blind prisoners fired their fatal
  mines?
  New realms, new worlds, exulting Science
    claims,
Still the dim future unexplored remains;
Her trembling scales the far-off planet weigh,
Her torturing prisms its elements betray, —
We know what ores the fires of Sirius melt,
What vaporous metals gild Orion's belt;
Angels, archangels, may have yet to learn
Those hidden truths our heaven-taught eyes discern;
Yet vain is Knowledge, with her mystic wand,
To pierce the cloudy screen and read beyond;
Once to the silent stars the fates were known,
To us they tell no secrets but their own.

At Israel's altar still we humbly bow,
But where, oh where, are Israel's prophets now?
Where is the sibyl with her hoarded leaves?
Where is the charm the weird enchantress
  weaves?
No croaking raven turns the auspex pale,
No reeking altars tell the morrow's tale;
The measured footsteps of the Fates are dumb,

Unseen, unheard, unheralded, they come,
Prophet and priest and all their following fail.
Who then is left to rend the future's veil?
  Who but the poet, he whose nicer sense
No film can baffle with its slight defence,
Whose finer vision marks the waves that stray,
Felt, but unseen, beyond the violet ray? —
Who, while the storm-wind waits its darkening
    shroud,
Foretells the tempest ere he sees the cloud, —
Stays not for time his secrets to reveal,
But reads his message ere he breaks the seal.
So Mantua's bard foretold the coming day
Ere Bethlehem's infant in the manger lay;
The promise trusted to a mortal tongue
Found listening ears before the angels sung.
So while his load the creeping pack-horse galled,
While inch by inch the dull canal-boat crawled,
Darwin beheld a Titan form " afar
Drag the slow barge or drive the rapid car,"
That panting giant fed by air and flame,
The mightiest forges task their strength to tame.

  Happy the poet! him no tyrant fact
Holds in its clutches to be chained and racked;
Him shall no mouldy document convict,
No stern statistics gravely contradict;
No rival sceptre threats his airy throne;
He rules o'er shadows, but he reigns alone.

Shall I the poet's broad dominion claim
Because you bid me wear his sacred name
For these few moments? Shall I boldly clash
My flint and steel, and by the sudden flash
Read the fair vision which my soul descries
Through the wide pupils of its wondering eyes?
List then awhile; the fifty years have sped;
The third full century's opened scroll is spread,
Blank to all eyes save his who dimly sees
The shadowy future told in words like these:

How strange the prospect to my sight appears,
Changed by the busy hands of fifty years!
Full well I know our ocean-salted Charles,
Filling and emptying through the sands and
    marls
That wall his restless stream on either bank,
Not all unlovely when the sedges rank
Lend their coarse veil the sable ooze to hide
That bares its blackness with the ebbing tide.
In other shapes to my illumined eyes
Those ragged margins of our stream arise:
Through walls of stone the sparkling waters
    flow,
In clearer depths the golden sunsets glow,
On purer waves the lamps of midnight gleam,
That silver o'er the unpolluted stream.
Along his shores what stately temples rise,
What spires, what turrets, print the shadowed
    skies!

Our smiling Mother sees her broad domain
Spread its tall roofs along the western plain;
Those blazoned windows' blushing glories tell
Of grateful hearts that loved her long and well;
Yon gilded dome that glitters in the sun
Was Dives' gift, — alas, his only one!
These buttressed walls enshrine a banker's name,
That hallowed chapel hides a miser's shame;
Their wealth they left, — their memory cannot fade
Though age shall crumble every stone they laid.

 Great lord of millions, — let me call thee great,
Since countless servants at thy bidding wait, —
Richesse oblige: no mortal must be blind
To all but self, or look at human kind
Laboring and suffering, — all its want and woe, —
Through sheets of crystal, as a pleasing show
That makes life happier for the chosen few
Duty for whom is something not to do.

 When thy last page of life at length is filled,
What shall thine heirs to keep thy memory build?
Will piles of stone in Auburn's mournful shade
Save from neglect the spot where thou art laid?
Nay, deem not thus; the sauntering stranger's eye
Will pass unmoved thy columned tombstone by,
No memory wakened, not a teardrop shed,
Thy name uncared for and thy date unread.

 But if thy record thou indeed dost prize,

Bid from the soil some stately temple rise, —
Some hall of learning, some memorial shrine,
With names long honored to associate thine :
So shalt thy fame outlive thy shattered bust
When all around thee slumber in the dust.
Thus England's Henry lives in Eton's towers,
Saved from the spoil oblivion's gulf devours;
Our later records with as fair a fame
Have wreathed each uncrowned benefactor's
    name;
The walls they reared the memories still retain
That churchyard marbles try to keep in vain.
In vain the delving antiquary tries
To find the tomb where generous Harvard lies:
Here, here, his lasting monument is found,
Where every spot is consecrated ground!
O'er Stoughton's dust the crumbling stone de-
    cays, —
Fast fade its lines of lapidary praise;
There the wild bramble weaves its ragged nets,
There the dry lichen spreads its gray rosettes;
Still in yon walls his memory lives unspent,
Nor asks a braver, nobler monument.
Thus Hollis lives, and Holden, honored, praised,
And good Sir Matthew, in the halls they raised;
Thus live the worthies of these later times,
Who shine in deeds, less brilliant, grouped in
    rhymes.
Say, shall the Muse with faltering steps retreat,
Or dare these names in rhythmic form repeat?

Why not as boldly as from Homer's lips
The long array of Argive battle-ships?
When o'er our graves a thousand years have
    past
(If to such date our threatened globe shall last)
These classic precincts, myriad feet have pressed,
Will show on high, in beauteous garlands dressed,
Those honored names that grace our later day, —
Weld, Matthews, Sever, Thayer, Austin, Gray,
Sears, Phillips, Lawrence, Hemenway, — to the
    list
Add Sanders, Sibley, — all the Muse has missed.

  Once more I turn to read the pictured page
Bright with the promise of the coming age.
Ye unborn sons of children yet unborn,
Whose youthful eyes shall greet that far-off
    morn,
Blest are those eyes that all undimmed behold
The sights so longed for by the wise of old.
  From high-arched alcoves, through resounding
    halls,
Clad in full robes majestic Science calls,
Tireless, unsleeping, still at Nature's feet,
Whate'er she utters fearless to repeat,
Her lips at last from every cramp released
That Israel's prophet caught from Egypt's priest.
  I see the statesman, firm, sagacious, bold,
For life's long conflict cast in amplest mould:
Not his to clamor with the senseless throng

That shouts unshamed, " Our party, right or
    wrong,"
But in the patriot's never-ending fight
To side with Truth, who changes wrong to right.
  I see the scholar; in that wondrous time
Men, women, children, all can write in rhyme.
These four brief lines addressed to youth in-
    clined
To idle rhyming in his notes I find:

*Who writes in verse that should have writ in
    prose*
Is like a traveller walking on his toes;
Happy the rhymester who in time has found
*The heels he lifts were made to touch the
    ground.*

  I see gray teachers, — on their work intent,
Their lavished lives, in endless labor spent,
Had closed at last in age and penury wrecked,
Martyrs, not burned, but frozen in neglect,
Save for the generous hands that stretched in
    aid
Of worn-out servants left to die half paid.
Ah, many a year will pass, I thought, ere we
Such kindly forethought shall rejoice to see, —
Monarchs are mindful of the sacred debt
That cold republics hasten to forget.
  I see the priest, — if such a name he bears
Who without pride his sacred vestment wears;

And while the symbols of his tribe I seek
Thus my first impulse bids me think and speak:

  Let not the mitre England's prelate wears
Next to the crown whose regal pomp it shares,
Though low before it courtly Christians bow,
Leave its red mark on Younger England's brow.
We love, we honor, the maternal dame,
But let her priesthood wear a modest name,
While through the waters of the Pilgrim's bay
A new-born Mayflower shows her keels the way.
Too old grew Britain for her mother's beads, —
Must we be necklaced with her children's creeds?
Welcome alike in surplice or in gown
The loyal lieges of the Heavenly Crown!
We greet with cheerful, not submissive, mien
A sister church, but not a mitred Queen!

A few brief flutters, and the unwilling Muse,
Who feared the flight she hated to refuse,
Shall fold the wings whose gayer plumes are shed,
Here where at first her half-fledged pinions spread.
  Well I remember in the long ago
How in the forest shades of Fontainebleau,
Strained through a fissure in a rocky cell,
One crystal drop with measured cadence fell.
Still, as of old, forever bright and clear,
The fissured cavern drops its wonted tear,

And wondrous virtue, simple folk aver,
Lies in that teardrop of *la roche qui pleure*.

  Of old I wandered by the river's side
Between whose banks the mighty waters glide,
Where vast Niagara, hurrying to its fall,
Builds and unbuilds its ever-tumbling wall;
Oft in my dreams I hear the rush and roar
Of battling floods, and feel the trembling shore,
As the huge torrent, girded for its leap,
With bellowing thunders plunges down the steep.
  Not less distinct, from memory's pictured urn,
The gray old rock, the leafy woods, return;
Robed in their pride the lofty oaks appear,
And once again with quickened sense I hear,
Through the low murmur of the leaves that stir,
The tinkling teardrop of *la roche qui pleure*.

So when the third ripe century stands complete,
As once again the sons of Harvard meet,
Rejoicing, numerous as the seashore sands,
Drawn from all quarters, — farthest distant lands,
Where through the reeds the scaly saurian steals,
Where cold Alaska feeds her floundering seals,
Where Plymouth, glorying, wears her iron crown,
Where Sacramento sees the suns go down;
Nay, from the cloisters whence the refluent tide
Wafts their pale students to our Mother's side, —
Mid all the tumult that the day shall bring,
While all the echoes shout, and roar, and ring,

These tinkling lines, oblivion's easy prey,
Once more emerging to the light of day,
Not all unpleasing to the listening ear
Shall wake the memories of this bygone year,
Heard as I hear the measured drops that flow
From the gray rock of wooded Fontainebleau.

Yet, ere I leave, one loving word for all
Those fresh young lives that wait our Mother's
    call:
  One gift is yours, kind Nature's richest
    dower, —
Youth, the fair bud that holds life's opening
    flower,
Full of high hopes no coward doubts enchain,
With all the future throbbing in its brain,
And mightiest instincts which the beating heart
Fills with the fire its burning waves impart.
  O joyous youth, whose glory is to dare, —
Thy foot firm planted on the lowest stair,
Thine eye uplifted to the loftiest height
Where Fame stands beckoning in the rosy light,
Thanks for thy flattering tales, thy fond deceits,
Thy loving lies, thy cheerful smiling cheats!
Nature's rash promise every day is broke, —
A thousand acorns breed a single oak,
The myriad blooms that make the orchard gay
In barren beauty throw their lives away;
Yet shall we quarrel with the sap that yields
The painted blossoms which adorn the fields,

When the fair orchard wears its May-day suit
Of pink-white petals, for its scanty fruit?
Thrice happy hours, in hope's illusion dressed,
In fancy's cradle nurtured and caressed,
Though rich the spoils that ripening years may
    bring,
To thee the dewdrops of the Orient cling, —
Not all the dye-stuffs from the vats of truth
Can match the rainbow on the robes of youth!

Dear unborn children, to our Mother's trust
We leave you, fearless, when we lie in dust:
While o'er these walls the Christian banner waves
From hallowed lips shall flow the truth that saves;
While o'er those portals *Veritas* you read
No church shall bind you with its human creed.
Take from the past the best its toil has won,
But learn betimes its slavish ruts to shun.
Pass the old tree whose withered leaves are shed,
Quit the old paths that error loved to tread,
And a new wreath of living blossoms seek,
A narrower pathway up a loftier peak;
Lose not your reverence, but unmanly fear
Leave far behind you, all who enter here!

As once of old from Ida's lofty height
The flaming signal flashed across the night,
So Harvard's beacon sheds its unspent rays
Till every watch-tower shows its kindling blaze.
Caught from a spark and fanned by every gale,

A brighter radiance gilds the roofs of Yale;
Amherst and Williams bid their flambeaus shine,
And Bowdoin answers through her groves of pine;
O'er Princeton's sands the far reflections steal,
Where mighty Edwards stamped his iron heel;
Nay, on the hill where old beliefs were bound
Fast as if Styx had girt them nine times round,
Bursts such a light that trembling souls inquire
If the whole church of Calvin is on fire!
Well may they ask, for what so brightly burns
As a dry creed that nothing ever learns?
Thus link by link is knit the flaming chain
Lit by the torch of Harvard's hallowed plain.

Thy son, thy servant, dearest Mother mine,
Lays this poor offering on thy holy shrine,
An autumn leaflet to the wild winds tost,
Touched by the finger of November's frost,
With sweet, sad memories of that earlier day,
And all that listened to my first-born lay.
With grateful heart this glorious morn I see, —
Would that my tribute worthier were of thee!

POST-PRANDIAL.

PHI BETA KAPPA.

WENDELL PHILLIPS, ORATOR; CHARLES GODFREY LELAND, POET.

1881.

"THE Dutch have taken Holland," — so the schoolboys used to say;
The Dutch have taken Harvard, — no doubt of that to-day!
For the Wendells were low Dutchmen, and all their vrows were Vans;
And the Breitmanns are high Dutchmen, and here is honest Hans.

Mynheers, you both are welcome! Fair cousin Wendell P.,
Our ancestors were dwellers beside the Zuyder Zee;
Both Grotius and Erasmus were countrymen of we,
And Vondel was our namesake, though he spelt it with a V.

It is well old Evert Jansen sought a dwelling over sea

On the margin of the Hudson, where he sampled
    you and me
Through our grandsires and great-grandsires, for
    you would n't quite agree
With the steady-going burghers along the Zuyder
    Zee.

Like our Motley's John of Barnveld, you have
    always been inclined
To speak, — well, — somewhat frankly, — to let
    us know your mind,
And the Mynheers would have told you to be cau-
    tious what you said,
Or else that silver tongue of yours might cost
    your precious head.

But we're very glad you've kept it; it was al-
    ways Freedom's own,
And whenever Reason chose it she found a royal
    throne;
You have whacked us with your sceptre; our
    backs were little harmed,
And while we rubbed our bruises we owned we
    had been charmed.

And you, our *quasi* Dutchman, what welcome
    should be yours
For all the wise prescriptions that work your
    laughter-cures?

"Shake before taking"? — not a bit, — the bottle-cure's a sham;
Take before shaking, and you'll find it shakes your diaphragm.

"Hans Breitmann gif a barty, — vhere is dot barty now?"
On every shelf where wit is stored to smooth the careworn brow!
A health to stout Hans Breitmann! How long before we see
Another Hans as handsome, — as bright a man as he!

THE FLANEUR.

BOSTON COMMON, DECEMBER 6, 1882.

DURING THE TRANSIT OF VENUS.

I LOVE all sights of earth and skies,
From flowers that glow to stars that shine;
The comet and the penny show,
All curious things, above, below,
Hold each in turn my wandering eyes:
I claim the Christian Pagan's line,
Humani nihil, — even so, —
And is not human life divine?

When soft the western breezes blow,
And strolling youths meet sauntering maids,
I love to watch the stirring trades
Beneath the Vallombrosa shades
Our much-enduring elms bestow;
The vender and his rhetoric's flow,
That lambent stream of liquid lies;
The bait he dangles from his line,
The gudgeon and his gold-washed prize.
I halt before the blazoned sign
That bids me linger to admire
The drama time can never tire,
The little hero of the hunch,

With iron arm and soul of fire,
And will that works his fierce desire, —
Untamed, unscared, unconquered Punch!
My ear a pleasing torture finds
In tones the withered sibyl grinds, —
The *dame sans merci's* broken strain,
Whom I erewhile, perchance, have known,
When Orleans filled the Bourbon throne,
A siren singing by the Seine.

But most I love the tube that spies
The orbs celestial in their march;
That shows the comet as it whisks
Its tail across the planets' disks,
As if to blind their blood-shot eyes;
Or wheels so close against the sun
We tremble at the thought of risks
Our little spinning ball may run,
To pop like corn that children parch,
From summer something overdone,
And roll, a cinder, through the skies.

Grudge not to-day the scanty fee
To him who farms the firmament,
To whom the milky way is free;
Who holds the wondrous crystal key,
The silent Open Sesame
That Science to her sons has lent;
Who takes his toll, and lifts the bar
That shuts the road to sun and star.

If Venus only comes to time,
(And prophets say she must and shall,)
To-day will hear the tinkling chime
Of many a ringing silver dime,
For him whose optic glass supplies
The crowd with astronomic eyes, —
The Galileo of the Mall.

Dimly the transit morning broke;
The sun seemed doubting what to do,
As one who questions how to dress,
And takes his doublets from the press,
And halts between the old and new.
Please Heaven he wear his suit of blue,
Or don, at least, his ragged cloak,
With rents that show the azure through!

I go the patient crowd to join
That round the tube my eyes discern,
The last new-comer of the file,
And wait, and wait, a weary while,
And gape, and stretch, and shrug, and smile,
(For each his place must fairly earn,
Hindmost and foremost, in his turn,)
Till hitching onward, pace by pace,
I gain at last the envied place,
And pay the white exiguous coin:
The sun and I are face to face;
He glares at me, I stare at him;
And lo! my straining eye has found

A little spot that, black and round,
Lies near the crimsoned fire-orb's rim.
O blessed, beauteous evening star,
Well named for her whom earth adores, —
The Lady of the dove-drawn car, —
I know thee in thy white simar;
But veiled in black, a rayless spot,
Blank as a careless scribbler's blot,
Stripped of thy robe of silvery flame, —
The stolen robe that Night restores
When Day has shut his golden doors, —
I see thee, yet I know thee not;
And canst thou call thyself the same?

A black, round spot, — and that is all;
And such a speck our earth would be
If he who looks upon the stars
Through the red atmosphere of Mars
Could see our little creeping ball
Across the disk of crimson crawl
As I our sister planet see.

And art thou, then, a world like ours,
Flung from the orb that whirled our own
A molten pebble from its zone?
How must thy burning sands absorb
The fire-waves of the blazing orb,
Thy chain so short, thy path so near,
Thy flame-defying creatures hear

The maelstroms of the photosphere!
And is thy bosom decked with flowers
That steal their bloom from scalding showers?
And hast thou cities, domes, and towers,
And life, and love that makes it dear,
And death that fills thy tribes with fear?

Lost in my dream, my spirit soars
Through paths the wandering angels know;
My all-pervading thought explores
The azure ocean's lucent shores;
I leave my mortal self below,
As up the star-lit stairs I climb,
And still the widening view reveals
In endless rounds the circling wheels
That build the horologe of time.
New spheres, new suns, new systems gleam;
The voice no earth-born echo hears
Steals softly on my ravished ears:
I hear them "singing as they shine" —
— A mortal's voice dissolves my dream:
My patient neighbor, next in line,
Hints gently there are those who wait.
O guardian of the starry gate,
What coin shall pay this debt of mine?
Too slight thy claim, too small the fee
That bids thee turn the potent key
The Tuscan's hand has placed in thine.
Forgive my own the small affront,

The insult of the proffered dime;
Take it, O friend, since this thy wont,
But still shall faithful memory be
A bankrupt debtor unto thee,
And pay thee with a grateful rhyme.

AVE.

PRELUDE TO "ILLUSTRATED POEMS."

FULL well I know the frozen hand has come
That smites the songs of grove and garden dumb,
And chills sad autumn's last chrysanthemum;

Yet would I find one blossom, if I might,
Ere the dark loom that weaves the robe of white
Hides all the wrecks of summer out of sight.

Sometimes in dim November's narrowing day,
When all the season's pride has passed away,
As mid the blackened stems and leaves we stray,

We spy in sheltered nook or rocky cleft
A starry disk the hurrying winds have left,
Of all its blooming sisterhood bereft:

Some pansy, with its wondering baby eyes —
Poor wayside nursling! — fixed in blank surprise
At the rough welcome of unfriendly skies;

Or golden daisy, — will it dare disclaim
The lion's tooth, to wear this gentler name?
Or blood-red salvia, with its lips aflame:

The storms have stripped the lily and the rose,
Still on its cheek the flush of summer glows,
And all its heart-leaves kindle as it blows.

So had I looked some bud of song to find
The careless winds of autumn left behind,
With these of earlier seasons' growth to bind.

Ah me! my skies are dark with sudden grief,
A flower lies faded on my garnered sheaf;
Yet let the sunshine gild this virgin leaf, —

The joyous, blessed sunshine of the past,
Still with me, though the heavens are overcast, —
The light that shines while life and memory last.

Go, pictured rhymes, for loving readers meant;
Bring back the smiles your jocund morning lent,
And warm their hearts with sunbeams yet unspent!

BEVERLY FARMS, *July* 24, 1884.

KING'S CHAPEL.

READ AT THE TWO HUNDREDTH ANNIVERSARY.

Is it a weanling's weakness for the past
   That in the stormy, rebel-breeding town,
Swept clean of relics by the levelling blast,
Still keeps our gray old chapel's name of
      "King's," —
Still to its outworn symbols fondly clings,
   Its unchurched mitres and its empty crown?

Poor harmless emblems! All has shrunk away
   That made them gorgons in the patriot's eyes;
The priestly plaything harms us not to-day;
The gilded crown is but a pleasing show,
An old-world heirloom, left from long ago,
   Wreck of the past that memory bids us prize.

Lightly we glance the fresh-cut marbles o'er;
   Those two of earlier date our eyes enthrall:
The proud old Briton's by the western door,
And hers, the Lady of Colonial days,
Whose virtues live in long-drawn classic
      phrase, —
   The fair Francesca of the southern wall.

Ay! those were goodly men that Reynolds drew,
   And stately dames our Copley's canvas holds,
To their old Church, their Royal Master, true,
Proud of the claim their valiant sires had earned,
That "gentle blood," not lightly to be spurned,
   Save by the churl ungenerous Nature moulds.

All vanished! It were idle to complain
   That ere the fruits shall come the flowers must
      fall;
Yet somewhat we have lost amidst our gain,
Some rare ideals time may not restore, —
The charm of courtly breeding, seen no more,
   And reverence, dearest ornament of all.

— Thus musing, to the western wall I came,
   Departing: lo! a tablet fresh and fair,
Where glistened many a youth's remembered
      name
In golden letters on the snow-white stone, —
Young lives these aisles and arches once have
      known,
   Their country's bleeding altar might not spare.

These died that we might claim a soil unstained,
   Save by the blood of heroes; their bequests
A realm unsevered and a race unchained.
Has purer blood through Norman veins come
      down

From the rough knights that clutched the Saxon's
  crown
    Than warmed the pulses in these faithful
      breasts?

These, too, shall live in history's deathless page,
  High on the slow-wrought pedestals of fame,
Ranged with the heroes of remoter age;
They could not die who left their nation free,
Firm as the rock, unfettered as the sea,
  Its heaven unshadowed by the cloud of shame.

While on the storied past our memory dwells,
  Our grateful tribute shall not be denied, —
The wreath, the cross of rustling immortelles;
And willing hands shall clear each darkening
    bust,
As year by year sifts down the clinging dust
  On Shirley's beauty and on Vassall's pride.

But for our own, our loved and lost, we bring
  With throbbing hearts and tears that still must
    flow,
In full-heaped hands, the opening flowers of
    spring,
Lilies half-blown, and budding roses, red
As their young cheeks, before the blood was shed
  That lent their morning bloom its generous
    glow.

Ah, who shall count a rescued nation's debt,
Or sum in words our martyrs' silent claims?
Who shall our heroes' dread exchange forget, —
All life, youth, hope, could promise to allure
For all that soul could brave or flesh endure?
They shaped our future; we but carve their names.

HYMN

FOR THE SAME OCCASION.

SUNG BY THE CONGREGATION TO THE TUNE OF TALLIS'S EVENING HYMN.

O'ERSHADOWED by the walls that climb,
   Piled up in air by living hands,
A rock amid the waves of time,
   Our gray old house of worship stands.

High o'er the pillared aisles we love
   The symbols of the past look down;
Unharmed, unharming, throned above,
   Behold the mitre and the crown!

Let not our younger faith forget
   The loyal souls that held them dear;
The prayers we read their tears have wet,
   The hymns we sing they loved to hear.

The memory of their earthly throne
   Still to our holy temple clings,
But here the kneeling suppliants own
   One only Lord, the King of kings.

FOR KING'S CHAPEL ANNIVERSARY.

Hark! while our hymn of grateful praise
   The solemn echoing vaults prolong,
The far-off voice of earlier days
   Blends with our own in hallowed song:

To Him who ever lives and reigns,
   Whom all the hosts of heaven adore,
Who lent the life His breath sustains,
   Be glory now and evermore!

HYMN. — THE WORD OF PROMISE,

(by supposition)

An Hymn set forth to be sung by the Great Assembly at Newtown, [Mass.] Mo. 12. 1. 1636.

[Written by OLIVER WENDELL HOLMES, eldest son of Rev. ABIEL HOLMES, eighth Pastor of the First Church in Cambridge, Massachusetts.]

LORD, Thou hast led us as of old
    Thine Arm led forth the chosen Race
Through Foes that raged, through Floods that roll'd,
    To Canaan's far off Dwelling-Place.

Here is Thy bounteous Table spread,
    Thy Manna falls on every Field,
Thy Grace our hungering Souls hath fed,
    Thy Might hath been our Spear and Shield.

Lift high Thy Buckler, Lord of Hosts!
    Guard Thou Thy Servants, Sons and Sires,
While on the Godless heathen Coasts
    They light Thine Israel's Altar-fires!

The salvage Wilderness remote
    Shall hear Thy Works and Wonders sung;

So from the Rock that Moses smote
  The Fountain of the Desert sprung.

Soon shall the slumbering Morn awake,
  From wandering Stars of Errour freed,
When Christ the Bread of Heaven shall break
  For Saints that own a common Creed.

The Walls that fence His Flocks apart
  Shall crack and crumble in Decay,
And every Tongue and every Heart
  Shall welcome in the new-born Day.

Then shall His glorious Church rejoice
  His Word of Promise to recall, —
One sheltering Fold, one Shepherd's Voice,
  One God and Father over all!

HYMN.

READ AT THE DEDICATION OF THE OLIVER WENDELL HOLMES HOSPITAL AT HUDSON, WISCONSIN, JUNE 7, 1887.

ANGEL of love, for every grief
   Its soothing balm thy mercy brings,
For every pang its healing leaf,
   For homeless want, thine outspread wings.

Enough for thee the pleading eye,
   The knitted brow of silent pain;
The portals open to a sigh
   Without the clank of bolt or chain.

Who is our brother? He that lies
   Left at the wayside, bruised and sore:
His need our open hand supplies,
   His welcome waits him at our door.

Not ours to ask in freezing tones
   His race, his calling, or his creed;
Each heart the tie of kinship owns,
   When those are human veins that bleed.

Here stand the champions to defend
   From every wound that flesh can feel;

Here science, patience, skill, shall blend
  To save, to calm, to help, to heal.

Father of Mercies! Weak and frail,
  Thy guiding hand Thy children ask;
Let not the Great Physician fail
  To aid us in our holy task.

Source of all truth, and love, and light,
  That warm and cheer our earthly days,
Be ours to serve Thy will aright,
  Be Thine the glory and the praise!

ON THE DEATH OF PRESIDENT GARFIELD.

I.

FALLEN with autumn's falling leaf
   Ere yet his summer's noon was past,
Our friend, our guide, our trusted chief, —
   What words can match a woe so vast!

And whose the chartered claim to speak
   The sacred grief where all have part,
Where sorrow saddens every cheek
   And broods in every aching heart?

Yet Nature prompts the burning phrase
   That thrills the hushed and shrouded hall,
The loud lament, the sorrowing praise,
   The silent tear that love lets fall.

In loftiest verse, in lowliest rhyme,
   Shall strive unblamed the minstrel choir, —
The singers of the new-born time,
   And trembling age with outworn lyre.

No room for pride, no place for blame, —
   We fling our blossoms on the grave,

Pale, — scentless, — faded, — all we claim,
This only, — what we had we gave.

Ah, could the grief of all who mourn
   Blend in one voice its bitter cry,
The wail to heaven's high arches borne
   Would echo through the caverned sky.

II.

O happiest land, whose peaceful choice
   Fills with a breath its empty throne!
God, speaking through thy people's voice,
   Has made that voice for once His own.

No angry passion shakes the state
   Whose weary servant seeks for rest;
And who could fear that scowling hate
   Would strike at that unguarded breast?

He stands, unconscious of his doom,
   In manly strength, erect, serene;
Around him Summer spreads her bloom;
   He falls, — what horror clothes the scene!

How swift the sudden flash of woe
   Where all was bright as childhood's dream!
As if from heaven's ethereal bow
   Had leaped the lightning's arrowy gleam.

Blot the foul deed from history's page;
   Let not the all-betraying sun
Blush for the day that stains an age
   When murder's blackest wreath was won.

III.

Pale on his couch the sufferer lies,
   The weary battle-ground of pain:
Love tends his pillow; Science tries
   Her every art, alas! in vain.

The strife endures how long! how long!
   Life, death, seem balanced in the scale,
While round his bed a viewless throng
   Await each morrow's changing tale.

In realms the desert ocean parts
   What myriads watch with tear-filled eyes,
His pulse-beats echoing in their hearts,
   His breathings counted with their sighs!

Slowly the stores of life are spent,
   Yet hope still battles with despair;
Will Heaven not yield when knees are bent?
   Answer, O Thou that hearest prayer!

But silent is the brazen sky;
   On sweeps the meteor's threatening train,
Unswerving Nature's mute reply,
   Bound in her adamantine chain.

Not ours the verdict to decide
  Whom death shall claim or skill shall save;
The hero's life though Heaven denied,
  It gave our land a martyr's grave.

Nor count the teaching vainly sent
  How human hearts their griefs may share, —
The lesson woman's love has lent,
  What hope may do, what faith can bear!

Farewell! the leaf-strown earth enfolds
  Our stay, our pride, our hopes, our fears,
And autumn's golden sun beholds
  A nation bowed, a world in tears.

THE GOLDEN FLOWER.

When Advent dawns with lessening days,
    While earth awaits the angels' hymn ;
When bare as branching coral sways
    In whistling winds each leafless limb ;
When spring is but a spendthrift's dream,
    And summer's wealth a wasted dower,
Nor dews nor sunshine may redeem, —
    Then autumn coins his Golden Flower.

Soft was the violet's vernal hue,
    Fresh was the rose's morning red,
Full-orbed the stately dahlia grew, —
    All gone ! their short-lived splendors shed.
The shadows, lengthening, stretch at noon ;
    The fields are stripped, the groves are dumb ;
The frost-flowers greet the icy moon, —
    Then blooms the bright chrysanthemum.

The stiffening turf is white with snow,
    Yet still its radiant disks are seen
Where soon the hallowed morn will show
    The wreath and cross of Christmas green ;
As if in autumn's dying days
    It heard the heavenly song afar,

And opened all its glowing rays,
 The herald lamp of Bethlehem's star.

Orphan of summer, kindly sent
 To cheer the fading year's decline,
In all that pitying Heaven has lent
 No fairer pledge of hope than thine.
Yes! June lies hid beneath the snow,
 And winter's unborn heir shall claim
For every seed that sleeps below
 A spark that kindles into flame.

Thy smile the scowl of winter braves
 Last of the bright-robed, flowery train,
Soft sighing o'er the garden graves,
 "Farewell! farewell! we meet again!"
So may life's chill November bring
 Hope's golden flower, the last of all,
Before we hear the angels sing
 Where blossoms never fade and fall!

NO TIME LIKE THE OLD TIME.

There is no time like the old time, when you and
    I were young,
When the buds of April blossomed, and the birds
    of spring-time sung!
The garden's brightest glories by summer suns
    are nursed,
But oh, the sweet, sweet violets, the flowers that
    opened first!

There is no place like the old place, where you
    and I were born,
Where we lifted first our eyelids on the splendors
    of the morn
From the milk-white breast that warmed us, from
    the clinging arms that bore,
Where the dear eyes glistened o'er us that will
    look on us no more!

There is no friend like the old friend, who has
    shared our morning days,
No greeting like his welcome, no homage like
    his praise:
Fame is the scentless sunflower, with gaudy
    crown of gold;
But friendship is the breathing rose, with sweets
    in every fold.

There is no love like the old love, that we courted
    in our pride;
Though our leaves are falling, falling, and we 're
    fading side by side,
There are blossoms all around us with the colors
    of our dawn,
And we live in borrowed sunshine when the day-
star is withdrawn.

There are no times like the old times, — they
    shall never be forgot!
There is no place like the old place, — keep
    green the dear old spot!
There are no friends like our old friends, — may
    Heaven prolong their lives!
There are no loves like our old loves, — God
    bless our loving wives!
  1865.

THE MORNING VISIT.

A sick man's chamber, though it often boast
The grateful presence of a literal toast,
Can hardly claim, amidst its various wealth,
The right unchallenged to propose a health;
Yet though its tenant is denied the feast,
Friendship must launch his sentiment at least,
As prisoned damsels, locked from lovers' lips,
Toss them a kiss from off their fingers' tips.

The morning visit, — not till sickness falls
In the charmed circles of your own safe walls;
Till fever's throb and pain's relentless rack
Stretch you all helpless on your aching back;
Not till you play the patient in your turn,
The morning visit's mystery shall you learn.

'T is a small matter, in your neighbor's case,
To charge your fee for showing him your face;
You skip up-stairs, inquire, inspect, and touch,
Prescribe, take leave, and off to twenty such.

But when at length by fate's transferred decree
The visitor becomes the visitee:
Oh, then, indeed, it pulls another string;
Your ox is gored, and that's a different thing!

Your friend is sick: phlegmatic as a Turk,
You write your recipe and let it work;
Not yours to stand the shiver and the frown,
And sometimes worse, with which your draught
    goes down.
Calm as a clock your knowing hand directs,
Rhei, jalapæ ana grana sex,
Or traces on some tender missive's back,
Scrupulos duos pulveris ipecac;
And leaves your patient to his qualms and
    gripes,
Cool as a sportsman banging at his snipes.

But change the time, the person, and the place,
And be yourself "the interesting case,"
You'll gain some knowledge which it's well to
    learn;
In future practice it may serve your turn.
Leeches, for instance, — pleasing creatures quite,
Try them, — and bless you, — don't you find
    they bite?
You raise a blister for the smallest cause,
But be yourself the sitter whom it draws,
And trust my statement, you will not deny
The worst of draughtsmen is your Spanish fly!
It's mighty easy ordering when you please
Infusi sennæ capiat uncias tres;
It's mighty different when you quackle down
Your own three ounces of the liquid brown.

Pilula, pulvis, — pleasant words enough,
When other throats receive the shocking stuff;
But oh, what flattery can disguise the groan
That meets the gulp which sends it through your
    own!
Be gentle, then, though Art's unsparing rules
Give you the handling of her sharpest tools;
Use them not rashly, — sickness is enough;
Be always "ready," but be never "rough."

Of all the ills that suffering man endures,
The largest fraction liberal Nature cures;
Of those remaining, 't is the smallest part
Yields to the efforts of judicious Art;
But simple *Kindness*, kneeling by the bed
To shift the pillow for the sick man's head,
Give the fresh draught to cool the lips that burn,
Fan the hot brow, the weary frame to turn, —
Kindness, untutored by our grave M. D.'s,
But Nature's graduate, whom she schools to
    please,
Wins back more sufferers with her voice and
    smile
Than all the trumpery in the druggist's pile.

Once more, be *quiet:* coming up the stair,
Don't be a plantigrade, a human bear,
But, stealing softly on the silent toe,
Reach the sick chamber ere you 're heard below.
Whatever changes there may greet your eyes,

THE MORNING VISIT.

Let not your looks proclaim the least surprise;
It's not your business by your face to show
All that your patient does not want to know;
Nay, use your optics with considerate care,
And don't abuse your privilege to stare.
But if your eyes may probe him overmuch,
Beware still further how you rudely touch;
Don't clutch his carpus in your icy fist,
But warm your fingers ere you take the wrist.
If the poor victim needs must be percussed,
Don't make an anvil of his aching bust;
(Doctors exist within a hundred miles
Who thump a thorax as they 'd hammer piles;)
If you must listen to his doubtful chest,
Catch the essentials, and ignore the rest.
Spare him; the sufferer wants of you and art
A track to steer by, not a finished chart.
So of your questions: don't in mercy try
To pump your patient absolutely dry;
He's not a mollusk squirming in a dish,
You 're not Agassiz, and he 's not a fish.

And last, not least, in each perplexing case,
Learn the sweet magic of a *cheerful face;*
Not always smiling, but at least serene,
When grief and anguish cloud the anxious scene.
Each look, each movement, every word and tone,
Should tell your patient you are all his own;
Not the mere artist purchased to attend,
But the warm, ready, self-forgetting friend,

THE MORNING VISIT.

Whose genial visit in itself combines
The best of cordials, tonics, anodynes.

Such is the *visit* that from day to day
Sheds o'er my chamber its benignant ray.
I give his health, who never cared to claim
Her babbling homage from the tongue of Fame;
Unmoved by praise, he stands by all confest,
The truest, noblest, wisest, kindest, best.
   1849.

HAIL, COLUMBIA!

1798.

THE FIRST VERSE OF THE SONG, BY JOSEPH HOPKINSON.

"Hail, Columbia! Happy land!
Hail, ye heroes, heaven-born band,
  Who fought and bled in Freedom's cause,
  Who fought and bled in Freedom's cause,
And when the storm of war was gone
Enjoy'd the peace your valor won.
  Let independence be our boast,
  Ever mindful what it cost;
  Ever grateful for the prize,
  Let its altar reach the skies.

"Firm — united — let us be,
Rallying round our Liberty;
As a band of brothers join'd,
Peace and safety we shall find."

. . . .

ADDITIONAL VERSES

WRITTEN AT THE REQUEST OF THE COMMITTEE FOR THE CONSTITUTIONAL CENTENNIAL CELEBRATION AT PHILADELPHIA, 1887.

Look our ransomed shores around,
Peace and safety we have found!

Welcome, friends who once were foes!
Welcome, friends who once were foes,
To all the conquering years have gained, —
A nation's rights, a race unchained!
  Children of the day new-born,
  Mindful of its glorious morn,
  Let the pledge our fathers signed
  Heart to heart forever bind!

    While the stars of heaven shall burn,
    While the ocean tides return,
    Ever may the circling sun
    Find the Many still are One!

Graven deep with edge of steel,
Crowned with Victory's crimson seal,
  All the world their names shall read!
  All the world their names shall read,
Enrolled with his, the Chief that led
The hosts whose blood for us was shed.
  Pay our sires their children's debt,
  Love and honor, nor forget
  Only Union's golden key
  Guards the Ark of Liberty!

    While the stars of heaven shall burn,
    While the ocean tides return,
    Ever may the circling sun
    Find the Many still are One!

Hail, Columbia ! strong and free,
Throned in hearts from sea to sea !
  Thy march triumphant still pursue !
  Thy march triumphant still pursue
With peaceful stride from zone to zone,
Till Freedom finds the world her own !
  Blest in Union's holy ties,
  Let our grateful song arise,
  Every voice its tribute lend,
  All in loving chorus blend !

   While the stars in heaven shall burn,
   While the ocean tides return,
   Ever shall the circling sun
   Find the Many still are One !

POEM

FOR THE DEDICATION OF THE FOUNTAIN AT STRATFORD-ON-AVON, PRESENTED BY GEORGE W. CHILDS, OF PHILADELPHIA.

WELCOME, thrice welcome is thy silvery gleam,
 Thou long-imprisoned stream!
Welcome the tinkle of thy crystal beads
As plashing raindrops to the flowery meads,
As summer's breath to Avon's whispering reeds!
From rock-walled channels, drowned in rayless
  night,
 Leap forth to life and light;
Wake from the darkness of thy troubled dream,
And greet with answering smile the morning's
  beam!

No purer lymph the white-limbed Naiad knows
 Than from thy chalice flows;
Not the bright spring of Afric's sunny shores,
Starry with spangles washed from golden ores,
Nor glassy stream Bandusia's fountain pours,
Nor wave translucent where Sabrina fair
 Braids her loose-flowing hair,
Nor the swift current, stainless as it rose
Where chill Arveiron steals from Alpine snows.

Here shall the traveller stay his weary feet
  To seek thy calm retreat;
Here at high noon the brown-armed reaper rest;
Here, when the shadows, lengthening from the
    west,
Call the mute song-bird to his leafy nest,
Matron and maid shall chat the cares away
  That brooded o'er the day,
While flocking round them troops of children
    meet,
And all the arches ring with laughter sweet.

Here shall the steed, his patient life who spends
  In toil that never ends,
Hot from his thirsty tramp o'er hill and plain,
Plunge his red nostrils, while the torturing rein
Drops in loose loops beside his floating mane ;
Nor the poor brute that shares his master's lot
  Find his small needs forgot, —
Truest of humble, long-enduring friends,
Whose presence cheers, whose guardian care defends!

Here lark and thrush and nightingale shall sip,
  And skimming swallows dip,
And strange shy wanderers fold their lustrous
    plumes
Fragrant from bowers that lent their sweet perfumes
Where Pæstum's rose or Persia's lilac blooms;

FOUNTAIN AT STRATFORD-ON-AVON.

Here from his cloud the eagle stoop to drink
    At the full basin's brink,
And whet his beak against its rounded lip,
His glossy feathers glistening as they drip.

Here shall the dreaming poet linger long,
    Far from his listening throng, —
Nor lute nor lyre his trembling hand shall bring;
Here no frail Muse shall imp her crippled wing,
No faltering minstrel strain his throat to sing!
These hallowed echoes who shall dare to claim
    Whose tuneless voice would shame,
Whose jangling chords with jarring notes would
    wrong
The nymphs that heard the Swan of Avon's song?

What visions greet the pilgrim's raptured eyes!
    What ghosts made real rise!
The dead return, — they breathe, — they live
    again,
Joined by the host of Fancy's airy train,
Fresh from the springs of Shakespeare's quickening brain!
The stream that slakes the soul's diviner thirst
    Here found the sunbeams first;
Rich with his fame, not less shall memory prize
The gracious gift that humbler wants supplies.

O'er the wide waters reached the hand that gave
    To all this bounteous wave, .

With health and strength and joyous beauty
    fraught;
Blest be the generous pledge of friendship,
    brought
From the far home of brothers' love, unbought!
Long may fair Avon's fountain flow, enrolled
    With storied shrines of old,
Castalia's spring, Egeria's dewy cave,
And Horeb's rock the God of Israel clave!

Land of our fathers, ocean makes us two,
    But heart to heart is true!
Proud is your towering daughter in the West,
Yet in her burning life-blood reign confest
Her mother's pulses beating in her breast.
This holy fount, whose rills from heaven descend,
    Its gracious drops shall lend, —
Both foreheads bathed in that baptismal dew,
And love make one the old home and the new!

August 29, 1887.

TO THE POETS WHO ONLY READ AND LISTEN.

When evening's shadowy fingers fold
    The flowers of every hue,
Some shy, half-opened bud will hold
    Its drop of morning's dew.

Sweeter with every sunlit hour
    The trembling sphere has grown,
Till all the fragrance of the flower
    Becomes at last its own.

We that have sung perchance may find
    Our little meed of praise,
And round our pallid temples bind
    The wreath of fading bays:

Ah, Poet, who hast never spent
    Thy breath in idle strains,
For thee the dewdrop morning lent
    Still in thy heart remains;

Unwasted, in its perfumed cell
    It waits the evening gale;
Then to the azure whence it fell
    Its lingering sweets exhale.

www.ingramcontent.com/pod-product-compliance
Lightning Source LLC
Chambersburg PA
CBHW031354160426
43196CB00007B/817